Tremors

poems by

Georgette Unis

Finishing Line Press
Georgetown, Kentucky

Tremors

Copyright © 2018 by Georgette Unis
ISBN 978-1-63534-664-0 First Edition
All rights reserved under International and Pan-American Copyright Conventions. No part of this book may be reproduced in any manner whatsoever without written permission from the publisher, except in the case of brief quotations embodied in critical articles and reviews.

ACKNOWLEDGMENTS

I would like to thank the editors of the following literary journals where these poems first appeared, sometimes in earlier versions.

California Quarterly: "Respect"
Poetry Quarterly: "The Performance"
Muddy River Poetry Review: "The End of Summer," "White Crepe Flowers"
The Homestead Review: "In Honor of a Certain Age," "Creep," "Medusa"
Plainsongs: "Seeker"
Sobotka Literary Magazine: "Warrior," "A Meditation"

I am deeply grateful to Richard Luftig for his support and guidance, to John Brantingham for his inspiration and encouragement, to R.T. Sedgwick for his critical evaluation, to the Ravens Poetry Workshop, and the many poets and friends who lent me their eyes and ears.

Publisher: Leah Maines
Editor: Christen Kincaid
Cover Art: Georgette Unis
Author Photo: Robert Walker
Cover Design: Elizabeth Maines McCleavy

Printed in the USA on acid-free paper.
Order online: www.finishinglinepress.com
   also available on amazon.com

Author inquiries and mail orders:
Finishing Line Press
P. O. Box 1626
Georgetown, Kentucky 40324
U. S. A.

Table of Contents

The Path 1
A Memoir in Eight Questions 2
A Cord 4
Desert Siblings 5
The Ever Presence 6
3 A. M. Umbrage 7
A Sierra Romance 9
In Want of Persephone 10
The Fish Hawks 11
August 12
Respect 14
Snow Swirl 15
The Performance 16
Medusa 17
Unsweetened 18
Sisyphus in Chef's Clothing or Chef Dreams
    of Retirement 19
A New Familiar 21
The End of Summer 22
Moon Over Mono Lake 24
Untended Tendril 25
Collateral Posting 26
Creep 27
In Honor of a Certain Age 28
Seeker 29
Family Trust 30
Warrior 31
White Crepe Flowers 32
A Meditation 33

The Path

An elder woman walks
beneath a row
of plum trees
whose blossoms
form a velvet carpet
as if she were a bride
on her way
to the altar.

An old man walks
with a cane
finely carved
in oak and
workday patterns.

He laughs
at sunrise,
welcomes
her breeze
as she enters
the park.

They join hands,
share coffee,
cake
and stories
until a canopy
of twilight
brings them home.

A Memoir in Eight Questions

He calls her on the land line
a small voice seven years wise
poised with a class assignment.

When you were my age, where did you live?
She spells the name slowly as he writes it down,

but she doesn't say how lonely a town it seemed
tucked into irrigation fields west of Phoenix.

What was your favorite book?
She says Nancy Drew Mysteries,

but she doesn't say anything about the locked school library
and how she had to beg the nuns to open it for her.

What music did you like?
That's easy, rock and roll, of course.

She almost says she loved her sister's piano concertos
and her brother's plaintive melodies on the clarinet
but not that she repeatedly set their metronome to faster beats.

What kind of phone did you have? Was it a cell?
How do you spell rotary?

She does not explain how she was taught to lie to unwanted callers
and lectured about a daughter's responsibility to protect her mother.

What was your favorite thing to do?
She tells him she loved to read but not that her other favorites

consisted of comic books about Wonder Woman and Superman,
Shakespeare classics and noir crime stories
she sneaked home from her father's store,

and how they mysteriously reappeared on the rack next day
along with her stash of candy bars she thought she hid.

What was your favorite TV show?
The Mickey Mouse Club she says

but not that her college age brother watched it more than she did
and how much she still misses his laughter and company.

What did you wear to school?
A dress and shoes and socks.

She doesn't tell him other children laughed at her ringlets,
accused her of wearing fire hoses on her head,

nor the oxfords that made her bump each foot into the other
so often her babysitter claimed she needed ballet lessons.

Last question, how did you get to your father's store?
Usually, she walked but didn't explain

she sometimes got off the bus in front of his building.
One day the bus driver told her father

she wasn't allowed to ride anymore because
she was playing horses and running down the aisle

waving her book bag strap as a lasso
to capture boredom, hog-tie it for branding and sale.

A Cord

Too weary to speak,
they gaze at each other.
The fire roars
in its screened cage
and heat flows
more than words.

A fragrance permeates
their living room
of an olive tree
taken down
some years ago
for logs
cured
in their yard,
its small branches
tied into bundles
of sprigs as tinder
when cold
would not abate
otherwise.

Desert Siblings
For Bruce Williams

Born in the shadow
of a date palm tree,
we learn to live
on cubed honey
and condensed milk.

Gilded sunsets float
as still life paintings
until wind transforms dust
into windshield pitting
grit.

Bone cold snow
and searing heat
do not prevent frost, bite
or sunburn.

They require
an understanding.

A fertile sea fossiled
these Mojave sands,
forested in ocotillo
and Joshua trees.
Wildflowers bloom here
after rare rains.

The Ever Presence

Four little bodies run
to and fro
as if the beach were
a race track
and they super engine cars

palm fronds wave
like checkered flags
cheering them on
louder than any crowd

but not them
in perpetual motion
along the sand
onto the pier
playing "Walk the Plank"

into the water
back onto the sand
handfuls of which fly
through the air
onto their backs
into their hair

onto the sand and the pier
turbos forever

until dinner.

3 A.M. Umbrage

The moth spins up
from behind my couch
into a lamp shade,
disappears again
over the edge
of a side table.

It flew in last weekend;
for three days
I try to kill it,
so tiny, so easy to crush.
Still, it taunts my swatter;
dances on its own wind.

Long before
a glimmer of dawn
or the warmth
of this summer morning,
it perches on a skylight
and waits.

As I try to lure the pest
to its demise
with a bright light
before it burrows in wool
and feeds its offspring
at my expense,

I dwell on our conversation,
its swirl of innuendos
in hope
of some insight
into our accusations
against each other,

but so far not enough
to settle who wounded whom,
nor enough kindling
to burn away
this pain.

A Sierra Romance

Before the rain
thunderstorm clouds build
on top of each other,
various shades of white and grey
in clichés of whipped cream
sullied by ash, a foreshadow
when lightning brings fires.

We hike among
hordes of mosquitos,
suffer bites through hair and shirts.
Thin air leaves us breathless
as do sweeping visions
of timeless granite lined
in yellow and green lichen.

We barely hear
whispers of thick pines
as torrents of water
race down gullies
over rocks and fallen logs,
a dance between sunlight
and shadow.

These mountains hold
a mother soul into which
we yearn to meld
as spirit, fly to each peak,
swoop into canyons,
catch wind drafts up rock walls,
coast along meadows,

kiss a purple lupine,
its life brief
as smoke crests the ridge.

In Want of Persephone

Leaves scatter
along roadways
when camellias bud
in December.

Instead of Demeter's
burnt earth,
my dry time feels
like the quiet cold
of a desert snow.

Sun rises east.
I wait at midday
watch west
for a spring melt
to spur wild flowers.

My daughter succumbs
to pomegranates.
Her young seedlings
charm me
in their need
for long cultivation.

Still I wonder
if time will ever
come for us
to tend each other
exclusively
again.

The Fish Hawks

A man enters the trail
in his sportsman vest,
carries his fly-fishing rod
as though it were as delicate
as a spider's web.

His two sons race ahead.
One pretends to cast a line.
The other scouts for sticks,
kicks dust and shouts,
waves magical swords
oblivious until
his father's hand sets him
on a trailside rock
for lessons in stealth.

The trio step lightly
as they descend
into the canyon below.
It cradles a stream
deep enough
for trout and the lure
of chipmunks
unaware that
osprey circle
the middle of sunlight
where raptors know
to disappear before
they capture prey
and fishermen mask
themselves in silence.

August

Morning clouds full of promise
against a passion of sunlight
cross high windows.

The quiet rush
of wind in aspen leaves
filters through the screen.

Mountain slopes
are coated in haze
while yellow light

warms the rocks,
tumbled and half-buried
in a stream

of fir and cedar branches,
dropped in sacrifice
to last winter's snows.

Hikers climb trails
adorned in surface roots,
sprayed with wild flowers

now beginning
their seasonal fade
and treasure

the last trickle
of snow melt
into a pine-needled earth.

Heat filters through the trees
and shadows thin
to a whitened afternoon

eager for showers
to moisten the rise
of late summer.

Respect

she leaves in early morning
it rains all day

wet grass at twilight

dreams tonight
of reaching

there are mountains
in the dark

I cannot see

only fear of stumbling
sustains my hesitation

to fly with open arms
to my daughter who climbs

beyond me

I want to say
remember dear one

I am she who taught you
to find your eagle's crag

but I dare not

some words are boulders

Snow Swirl

Tracks of little ovals
line the trail,
too small for a child,
too smooth for paws,
a mystery until
the dog appears
in snug boots,
a red bandana
around his neck,
talisman of affection.

For a moment,
I think if I could be
that furry creature,
I would roll on my back
in the soft confection,
draw circles with my head
and bark snowflakes
into my mouth.

Instead, they walk
side by side.
He doesn't scamper
in the deep snow
but swishes his tail
as if that says it all.

The Performance

They bloom in a burst of colors
translucent, intense, delicate
Degas ballerinas taking a bow.
They remind me of her clusters of flowers,
her dramatic display of inhaling their fragrance
as if she were playing to the uppermost tier
of an amphitheater.

She commanded me many times
to write about her life, her memoir.
With eyes of a playful but hungry child,
she drew me into her whirls where
I nearly drowned.
Her epics would pirouette
as a snaked river at each telling,
yet were always the same flow:
she at center stage a victim
blameless and resourceful
outsmarting her villains.

In the midst of a migraine one night
the word *quotidian* persisted
while my swollen brain ached
with memories of our daily life
and bread she often baked for me,
delectable when fresh from oven to table,
dripping in butter and succor.

Both of us unaware then
those afternoon stories would leave
a stringent aftertaste lingering
like the smell of vinegar
I use to release hard water stains
remnants of many bouquets
in my glass vase for roses.

Medusa

Her hair droops,
the strands
almost tangled
but not wild
as she waters mint
in the cool morning.

Roots
in her rose garden
begin to wither
from underwatered soil.
Her husband
dismisses flowers
as hybrids of nature,
insists on herbs,
medicinal, hardy,
worth the water.

Each curl extends,
writhes on her head.
when she lifts
her face to him.
He catches his breath,
becomes the canyon wall
around her.

Unsweetened

You come around like a carousel.
I buy your wedding dress
and the circle widens.
With each accoutrement:
career
husband
child
home
pet
the music slows
until I barely hear the notes
and we rarely ride our horses
side by side.

Whose proscription is this?
We know our offspring
never fully separate.
I see my mother's smile
in the mirror,
hear her voice
in a song:
physics
and metaphysics
are one.

Sisyphus in Chef's Clothing or Chef Dreams of Retirement

He chooses fresh artichokes,
shallots, mushrooms
and pounds of lamb,
loads them into his cart,
perspires heavily
as he pushes it uphill
to his kitchen.

In the back garden
he harvests thyme,
rosemary, fennel
and fantasies
of the final meal
he will command.

All day he carves meat,
chops herbs
and vegetables,
steams mussels
and monk fish,
simmers sauces
over gas burners,
a chef's hat low
on his brow.

At dinner he serves
several courses
from this morning's cache,
a grand Marnier soufflé,
dark chocolate truffles,
a crisp sauvignon blanc,
robust cabernets,
and as a farewell gesture,

a selection of ports
to his wealthy guests
who savor each morsel
after which they
slumber in bliss.

They call him
the next morning
for evening reservations.

A New Familiar

A shepherd dog
stands in snow
while his eyes watch me
through an open
window.

Though this is not
my house yet
I beckon him
into the mud room
among boots and
make a bed of coats
for enough shelter
to keep him near
content.

Still his gaze
is steady
patient
expecting
as evening begins
a requirement
for supper.

Water is
an easy flow
from tap to bowl
but food
presents
a dilemma.

The End of Summer

The blaze kindles another
and another and, in turn,
each ignites more until
they coat the clouds
in orange dust
brilliant at sunset
as though a league of dragons
breathe flames across the sky.

All night our windows rattle
in the congregation of Sierra winds
and fierce energy
as aspen and pine disintegrate
like medieval heretics
whose only sin—their existence.
By morning, a burnt haze
shrouds the sun
and smoke infiltrates our lungs.
Everything tastes bitter.

For a brief respite between storms
I examine the tip of a fir tree, a triad
of one long stem supported by two others
where we once placed an angel,
homemade out of a light bulb and paper gown,
when my brother lived and our children were young.

Our families shared these mountains
on holidays and long vacations.
We hiked the forest trails with promises
of chocolate bars at the summit
and hot cocoa after ski adventures.

Time consumes our past slowly
as in a daily meal
we give to a tame pet
but these uncontrolled burnings
devour our history
like a ravenous beast,
with barely a moment to capture it.

Moon Over Mono Lake

Back county hikers
at my door,
their dream of John Muir Trail
frozen as the snow
covering it;
they share tales
of new waterfalls
from multiple streams,
flooded meadows uncrossable,
damaged campgrounds closed.

We console ourselves
in a trek to this ancient lake,
for our ritual worship
when the full moon
fills its reflection
in a stream of light
over dark waters
and hides
calcite landscapes,

but not a great horned owl,
who prowls his full-feathered body
seen only as a flash of white down
as it sups on a careless
ground squirrel.

Meanwhile, mosquitoes feast
on our exposed ankles,
a reminder we must pay
summer dues
even before
it arrives.

Untended Tendril

When conversation turns
to talk of their mother,
the elderly sisters hesitate,
wary of how memories unfold
as a film stutters its images
on a worn projector
hardly available anymore.

Habits of home,
husband and children
mired her aspirations
in well fertilized soil
with stories of a sapling
trimmed too soon,
of college degrees
and a career pruned
so they can have
their accomplishments,
which she proudly wore
as corsages
even if the pearl-tipped pins
pierced her skin.

As executors, they manage
the plum orchards,
but for too many years
they cover each of her cuts
with a mental tree tar.
No matter the Buddha
in their garden,
they cannot sand callouses,
nor allow the sap to weep.

Collateral Posting

Red clay in heavy bags
beckon as a thorn in my palm.
It wants images
though the color stains
my hands, tools, nailbrush.
Its iron eats into my skin,
bloodies my plaster molds.

Distortions smear pieces,
leave some eyes lifeless
and some faces without identity,
but I am a sent missile
with no time for the personal.

The forms do not disappear into ashes
as cremated bodies
nor do they explode in the kiln.
They become vitrified reminders,
death masks of unrecorded people,
in semblance to misshapen produce,
discounted for quick sale.

I form sixty images, each one
to represent several thousand people
though that barely covers the toll
from a war enamored with itself,
death no longer the province
of a particular ethnicity.

The faces hang on my wall
for years, become kinsmen
until sadness permeates
my skin, bone, curdles marrow.
I pack the masks in boxes
beneath my work table,
a crypt for relics
of a sacramental union.

Creep

The weeds thrive again
lush with bright green leaves,
jagged and tough,
not as tasty as the new mint
or tender as berginia, both of which
feed an entire neighborhood
of voracious insects.
An army of lizards
will not be enough
to protect my garden.

Nothing eats the weeds.
Maybe some goats
or perhaps some rabbits,
but they will eat
everything else first.
With no other natural predators,
just humans with herbicides
against which the weeds
mutate resistance,
they flourish.

I read that cockroaches
will inherit the earth
after humans extinguish themselves.
I imagine they will scamper
over tattered pages of essays
on the merits of organic gardening.
Weeds will slither their roots hungrily
into our remains and sprout fields
of yellow dandelions
in memoriam.

In Honor of a Certain Age

They open just enough to tease
hope of a week's survival,
an expensive dozen roses,
sent as a token of affection,
the bouquet presented
in an arranged marriage
of décor by a florist.

The garden rose glories in moonlight,
her petals unfurl in velvet colors,
transparent and opaque all at once
like a Rothko painting,
seductive on a continuum
from bud to full petal bow,

akin to a woman who lives
in the city exposed.
She requires we wear gloves
because she wears thorns
and razor-edge leaves.
Lured by her fragrance,
if we pluck her, we pay.

No wax paper pressings here
into keepsake books.

But the wild rose deserves honor
as Lilith of her species, the original
whose vines climb
wherever they choose
and whose branches gather
into a hedge of untainted blooms.

Cherished by Van Gogh,
her portrait hangs
on his museum wall.

Seeker

The woman asks about mystics.
I steer our conversation
to the hybridization of roses,
concepts of metaphor,
texture in relationship.

She persists
as a documenter,
a journalist who meditates
on spiritual weavings
that cradle her world.

When I offer figs,
she purses her lips,
so I recommend she read
Rumi and Hafiz who suggest
the pathways are prescribed

by sacred writings spoken
in isolation, in repetition,
sometimes in song
and with much patience,
though I am in no manner kindred.

Glimpses of the Great Unknowable
come to me in flower petals.

Family Trust

We talk blithely
about procedures
to remove
each other's name
from deeds
and documents
as though death
doesn't scan
like a raptor
of opportunity.

As I follow you
up the stairs
to begin
our day's routine,
I watch you
grown tentative
as a hare
anticipating night.

Warrior

Coffee steam rises
through a clatter of images
from your late morning sleep,
or rather oversleep.
Such phantoms linger
all day as you claim
an infertile dawn.

I listen for awhile
to your cherished anger,
but we both know
it takes a leonine feat
to meld our swords
with blossoms,
seductive and fragrant
as a skein of jasmine,
after flaying one's soul
for the sake of mark-making
on a canvas
or a sheet of paper.

Tonight, the fountain will whisper
crystal water over its stones.
We will drink our wine
in its courtyard and talk
of quiet imperatives,
how they require
more expertise
than flailing arms.

We will talk about bearded elders
who chant and dance around
the burning of old manuscripts.
And we will talk about
the Buddhist monk
who defeats your warrior
drenched in last night's dreams.

White Crepe Flowers

In war zones everywhere
people continue to die
but all I have to offer
are white crepe flowers
from the sentinel bush
in front of my window.

Cold in winter
and warm in summer,
once part of my garden,
then a garage and finally, a studio,
this room needs covers on its skylights
with sun-resistant screens
because their cobwebs
don't protect me
from constant exposure.

Now its tiled floor
and open shutters
welcome the fragrance
of lavender and orange blossoms
all the way into deep winter.

Here, I read the newspaper,
watch television and dwell
on the evergreen plant as it guards
like a village grandmother,
round and wide,
its white petals crinkled, transparent
as an old woman's skin.

My blooms don't always fall
to the ground when their cycle ends.
Sometimes they disappear as though
their presence becomes a mirage
when hope is fragile.

A Meditation

Wild grasses glisten in the meadow,
bend to a rush of wind through thick pines,

the sound more mother to me than ocean waves;
the Sierras present a same timelessness.

I hear his breath as we reach the trail's crest,
ghosts of his father and grandfather

on each shoulder, the sins of nature
a backpack of stones in his male line.

We come to this idyllic scene,
to consider the outcome of his illness,

its contest between remission and terminal
and its effect on his young sons.

Belief holds power. Still, doubt seeps in the way
snow-melt crevices earth, slow and insidious.

Thundershowers this afternoon soften the heat
and cast our mountains in cinematic silver light.

Ancient peoples would think gods reside in such a place
when iridescent streaks flash from clouds to land,

ignite fires and leave blackened trunks as tombstones,
decades old, along some favorite hikes.

When alpine-glow highlights the trees and mountainsides,
we wrap ourselves in the promise of tomorrow's sunrise

and afternoon rains that settle dust, aware
the answer promises everything, and nothing.

Georgette Unis was born and raised in Arizona. Upon moving to California, she fell in love with the Eastern Sierras where she spends weeks at a time. She has an MFA in mixed media painting. She made her profession as a painter and ceramic sculptor with several solo and group exhibitions, some of which included broadsides of her poems.

Her poetry is published in *Muddy River Poetry Review, Sobotka Literary Magazine, The Homestead Review, Plainsongs* and various other journals. Through the art of writing, she explores the complex relationships between people, often within the natural settings of mountain forests, deserts and urban gardens.

She maintains her studio and home in Southern California where she lives with her husband of forty-seven years.

www.ingramcontent.com/pod-product-compliance
Lightning Source LLC
LaVergne TN
LVHW041504070426
835507LV00012B/1321